#15

A Day Above

STAMFORD

Christine C. Nowell

Photography by John J. Nowell *FRGS LRPS*

Foreword

I am honoured to be writing a brief foreword to this fascinating book. Flying over Stamford has given John Nowell the opportunity to photograph this unique town from an entirely different perspective to that which is familiar to those on the ground. Seen through a car windscreen, much of Stamford is hidden and it is easy to miss the narrow medieval lanes and alleys that still alongside Victorian and Geo terraces. The lives of past generations can be guessed at when their habitats are seen from the air. Good photography unlocks a sense of place, often swept aside by busy lives. The views in this book are breathtaking and enable us to pause, step back and appreciate our built heritage and natural surroundings a little more.

Lady Victoria Leatham, Burghley House, Stamford.

Lady Victoria and Leslie Law, holding the actual Olympic Gold Medal that was awarded to Lord Burghley at the 1928 Amsterdam Olympics, when he won the 400 yard hurdles event. Leslie Law won his Gold Medal at the 2004 Athens Olympics.

A Day Above
STAMFORD

Christine C. Nowell
Photography by John J. Nowell *FRGS LRPS*

Published by:

Zodiac Publishing UK Ltd
Companies House 5330249
65 Deans Street, Oakham
Rutland LE15 6AF
United Kingdom
e mail general@zodiacpublishing.org
www.zodiacpublishing.co.uk

First published 1st January 2007

ISBN 978-1-904566-60-X

Design by William A. Nowell.
Edited by Simone J. Nowell.
Scanning by Gildenburgh Media Solutions.
Printed by Gutenburg Press, Malta.

See page 128 for other books in the series.

Contents

Front cover: View from the spire of All Saints Church.
Front end paper: Sunrise at the disused windmill at Ketton.
Page 1: The splendid Coat of Arms of Stamford.
Page 2/3: View from Lion Bridge towards Burghley House.
Page 4/5: Reflections of the River Welland beneath Town Bridge.

Page 6/7: Aerial view of Stamford from the south.
Page 8/9: Winter reflections across the Meadows.
Page 10/11: Ruins of Wothorpe House on a frosty morning.
Rear end paper: Sunset on the River Welland.
Back cover: A caravan rally in the grounds of Burghley House.

Introduction by John Judge, former Mayor of Stamford.

Stamford is a town of ordered antiquity. Over the past 2000 years a dramatic series of events have left their mark on the town. As the former Mayor, as part of my official duties, it has been my privilege, and an object of fascination, to examine the many artifacts, both in the Mayor's parlour and in the town archives. The modern visitor might think that Stamford, a relatively small, rural market town in the lower limb of the county of Lincolnshire, would hardly figure in any study of English history. I can tell you that this is not so, for when it comes to Stamford, there are many fascinating historical tales to tell and delights to see. A stroll around this beautiful, old market town is easily the best way to enjoy its charms.

The first phase of events that were to shape the town, occurred during the time of the Roman invasion. Local stone slabs were laid in the alluvial beds of the River Welland to ease the crossing for Roman legions marching north. This modest feat of engineering gave the town its name, the place once known as 'Stone Ford' eventually became Stamford. During their 400 hundred year stay the Romans built a camp at Casterton Major, just north of Stamford, to act as a supply point on Ermine Street, the newly built London to York road. In AD 61 the Celtic tribes, led by Queen Boadicea Victoria (a name given to her by the Romans) rebelled, and pursued the IXth Legion across their own 'Stone Ford' on the River Welland. The victory was only temporary however, as the well-disciplined Roman troops soon defeated Queen Boudicca and her combined Celtic force.

Under Saxon rule, the town of Stamford developed around the streets that still exist today. Such was the importance of the town that when the Normans invaded in 1066, they built a castle here to protect their newly acquired kingdom. The town prospered rapidly and with it came the building of many fine churches. All Saints, St Mary's, St George's and St Martin's were built during this prosperous time and, in addition, many other religious orders arrived in Stamford to build colleges, schools and houses. St Leonard's Priory still stands and near Stamford School is Brasenose Gate - believed to belong to an embryo university formed temporarily by dissatisfied members of Oxford University. Brasenose was originally founded by King Henry VIII and is considered to be one of the best colleges in Oxford. These Stamford students were soon forced to return to Oxford and the original knocker of the gate is now in the main hall at Brasenose College.

During the 15th century, the wool trade developed rapidly. Forests surrounding the town were felled to provide timber for the growing navy of King Henry VIII and large numbers of sheep were soon able to graze on the newly exposed land. This phase of prosperity continued throughout the reign of Queen Elizabeth I who, as a reward, granted the manor of Stamford to her Lord High Treasurer, Lord Burghley.

By the 18th century, coach traffic was increasing throughout England. Stamford, located on the Great North Road, 100 miles from London, became a major focal point in the kingdom, as both a business and social centre. The Assembly Rooms and Theatre, surrounded by elegant Georgian houses, were at the heart of Stamford's social centre. These elegant, well preserved buildings make Stamford the unique stone-built market town it is today with 600 listed buildings.

The approach from the south into Stamford has changed little in the past 200 years. The road passes the imposing entrance to Burghley Park known as the 'Bottle Lodges'. Just past this entrance, the town sign invites the visitor to 'stay awhile amidst its charms'. At the top of High Street St Martin's, is the Lady Anne Hotel with its charming gardens and almost opposite is the Garden House Hotel with its gardens hidden behind the building. Further down on the right is Stamford Girls School and the old coaching inn, the Bull and Swan. It was this picturesque view that so captivated both J.M.W. Turner and Walter Scott that they both 'stayed awhile' to paint the scene. On each side of the road are 17th century Georgian and Regency houses dominated by the tower of St Martin's Church, built in 1430. Here monuments to the Cecil family may be seen, including the great tomb of Lord Burghley who died in 1598. At the bottom of the hill is the George Hotel built in 1728, perhaps the most famous coaching inn in England, where once more that sixty coaches stopped each day. The 18th century journey from London to Stamford took twelve hours, a remarkable everyday feat considering the state of the roads two hundred years ago.

At the bottom of the hill the road crosses the Welland via Town Bridge. From either side of the bridge the view is enchanting. Downriver one can see to the foot bridge, upriver the Meadows and ahead up the hill is the towering beauty of St Mary's spire, which, for the technically minded, is a 14th century broach spire built upon a 13th century tower. To the right is the splendid Town Hall built in 1776 by the noted architect Lovell and opposite are timber framed houses with a fascinating selection of shops at ground level.

St Mary's Hill turns left and becomes St Mary's Street with many fine 19th century shops separated by mysterious, narrow passageways such as Old Barn Passage,

Cross Keys Lane, Bugle Lane and Gooches Court, all of which lead down to the river. The road - and this was the Great North Road only 40 years ago - turns right into St John's Street, dominated by the 15th century St John's Church and then enters Red Lion Square. The 13th century, All Saint's Church overlooks the square where on two days of the week parking places are replaced by market stalls. Several interesting streets radiate from the square, including Barn Hill where at number 9, King Charles I spent his last night of freedom.

From Red Lion Square the road goes uphill along Red Lion Street and into Broad Street. On the left is Browne's Hospital, an almshouse founded by Browne, Merchant of the Staple at Calais and a worthy of Stamford, who died in 1489. The hospital was founded for eleven needy souls, ten men and one woman, who lived in cubicles within the main building. In 1870 changes were made and a courtyard surrounded by separate cottages was built and occupied. Elegant houses, many now offices and shops, line Broad Street. The Roman Catholic Church, built in 1864 on the site of the old Dolphin pub sits some way up the street. On the opposite side is Stamford Museum, formerly the School of Arts, built in 1894. Towards the end of Broad Street, just before the road turns right into Star Lane, is the renamed Lord Burghley public house. Further along, at the end of Star Lane by the Half Moon, the road turns left into St Paul's Street and past Stamford School with its broad lawn, clock tower and chapel which was originally part of St Paul's Church. Across the road from the school is the remnant of Brasenose Gate and behind the wall, in the gardens, is a small plinth dedicated to the Polish soldiers of the 1st Independent Parachute Brigade stationed in and around Stamford, many of whom lost their lives in Allied operations during World War II.

In the opposite direction the road opens up into the pedestrianised High Street. Halfway down is the Tuscan portico of the Stamford Public Library. Opposite the library is Maiden Lane which leads down to St George's Square and the 13th century St George's Church. In the far corner of the square are the original Assembly Rooms, built in 1760 in the social heyday of Stamford. At the corner of the square and St Mary's Street is the Stamford Arts Centre and restored theatre. This part of the town was recently transformed into a film set for Pride & Prejudice (see page 58) and for a while the town was filled with actors and extras in the colourful costumes of that period. The arts centre not only houses many fascinating exhibitions but is also home to the well-stocked and well-informed Tourist Information Centre. A popular coffee shop provides a welcome respite for both tourists and visitors alike. Whilst the refurbished theatre screens a variety of the latest films, providing a much appreciated entertainment centre. Along St Mary's Street, past the half timbered St Mary's Vaults public house is the imposing, colonnaded frontage of the old Stamford Hotel, now containing a wide variety of shops and businesses. The road continues across the top of St Mary's hill and on to St Mary's Street with its tantalizing shops and unusual eating places. It then continues on and down into Castle Street then up again to Sheep Market, which used to be filled to capacity with sheep during market days, and then on to St Peter's Hill. This was the original location of the Norman castle, now cleared to make way for the bus station. Further along this road at Petergate, the last bastion of the old town gate still stands indicating what once was the edge of this now sprawling town. A little further along on the right stands the elegant, regency styled 'Rutland Terrace' with its extensive view over the river valley.

The road turns left and descends into Austin Street which bears round to the left then turns right before descending further on to the cobbled, leafy Kings Mill Lane. This leads down to the river where the old Kings Mill has been converted into apartments. The footbridge across the river leads on to the grassed area known as the Meadows. A pathway on the right leads to the Freemens Meadow and a plinth marks the point where the original Roman 'Stone Ford' was laid. The scene from here and back along the river bank is, in my opinion, the most delightful view of the town.

The Maltings and Water Street run from the Town Bridge, along the south side of the river and continues right into Newtown, over the railway bridge and into Burghley Park. The easy walk from Town Bridge to Burghley House takes less than twenty minutes. The approach to Burghley House was created by the famous landscape gardener 'Capability' Brown and today this is often complimented by the herd of fallow deer. (See page 112). The tour of Burghley House is a complete book on its own, especially the world renowned paintings. Afternoon tea in the Orangery, with its delightful views over the gardens, is a treat not to be missed.

An alternative to walking, or seeing Stamford by car, is to drift over the town in a hot-air balloon. As the balloon ascends above the Meadows, the passengers see Stamford from a completely different perspective. Another option is a flight over the town in a Tiger Moth. A ride in this two-seater biplane, is an adventure with a magnificent view. For those not able to fly over Stamford, this book offers a memorable bird's eye view of the best stone town in England. Stamford not only welcomes you to stay awhile but to come again.

Mayor John H. Judge,
The Town Hall,
Stamford.

Chapter 1

DAWN

6 am

The minute hand of the Burghley Golf Club clock ticks past 6 am as the first golden rays of the rising sun reflect from its black face. Even before the sun has risen above the horizon, balloonists have been testing their propane burners, firing long plumes of orange flames into the lightening sky. The balloons are initially inflated with cold air followed by bursts of hot flames. Hot air expands and the balloons 'stand up' ready for take off. Pilots complete their checks, the passengers embark and the balloons are ready to take off just as the sun appears above the horizon - the start of another 'Day Above Stamford'.

6.15 am

The gentle light of a new dawn warms the herd of deer in Burghley Park while St Paul's Street is completely deserted and devoid of cars. On the Meadows, by the River Welland, the flaming roar of the propane burner heralds the final preparation of the balloons before take-off.

6.30 am

A youngster chases the long shadows across the Meadows. The new, bright light illuminates the balloons straining but waiting for the first flight of the day.

6.45 am

By 6.45 am the first balloon is floating above Stamford. Near the ruins of Wothorpe House, a solitary tree stands above the frost-covered grazing. Once this area marked the northerly edge of Rockingham Forest but the trees were felled and the wood used to build new ships for the navy of King Henry VIII.

7 am

More than 100 years before Bleriot flew across the English Channel, gas-filled balloons were flying over England. At the same time as these gas balloons were flying, Sheepmarket Street was filled to capacity with sheep waiting to be sold. The modern Virgin balloon is also filled to capacity as it lifts off from the Meadows, just a short walk from Sheepmarket. The balloons climb up into the bright morning sky to drift with the wind to an unknown destination.

Graham booke

7.15 am

Where the castle once stood, daffodils bloom in front of recently restored houses. Inset at left, the ancient village of Barnack lies four miles to the southeast of Stamford. The undulating grasslands to the west of the village are the remains of the limestone quarries first used by the Romans almost 2000 years ago. The limestone was formed from sea shells during the Jurassic Period, 20 million years ago when a warm shallow sea covered the area. Quarrying continued into the Middle Ages when stone from Barnack was used to build both Ely and Peterborough Cathedrals. The vast area is now home to wild flowers and the Chalkhill Blue and White Marbled butterflies. Also carefully restored is this De Havilland Tiger Moth waiting for its first flight of the day.

7.30 am

The area around Stamford has been renowned for agriculture since Roman times. In the 1800s, mechanised agriculture developed with the introduction of the traction engine. During World War II, members of the Women's Land Army filled places left by male farm workers, who had left to serve on the front line. At Essendine, where thousands of tractors were produced during WWII, a modern industrial park has developed in the extensive former railway yards.   In the 1930s, the Mallard steam train gained the unbeaten world speed record along this track.

7.45 am

From the balloon, the graceful spire of the church at Uffington rises above the surrounding trees near the old entrance to the original home of the Bertie family, who were great patrons of Stamford. They presented the great mace, the majestic punchbowl and much of the corporation plates which are now on display in the Mayor's Parlour. At Uffington, an early Saxon site, a 6th century funeral urn was found during the construction of the Stamford-Essendine railway line.

8 am

The early morning mist continues to burn off as the sun's rays gain strength. The parish church, situated at the most northerly point of Easton-on-the-Hill, looks out and across the Welland Valley towards Stamford. Near the church is a popular location known as the Priests House, now owned by the National Trust and open to the public. This is a favourite stopping point for walkers on the long distance footpath called 'The Jurrasic Way'. The footpath roughly follows the Welland Valley from Harringworth, in Northamptonshire, through Easton-on-the-Hill, before descending into the valley again to pass through the Meadows to reach the George Hotel in Stamford, where travellers have been stopping for hundreds of years.

8.15 am

The area to the south of the River Welland was first mentioned in the Anglo-Saxon Chronicle. In 918 AD King Edward of Wessex built a fortress on the south bank of the river to support his attacks on the Danish invaders. Today, this area, sometimes known as 'Stamford Baron', is the district of Wothorpe which developed in size through the ages as Stamford itself became more crowded.

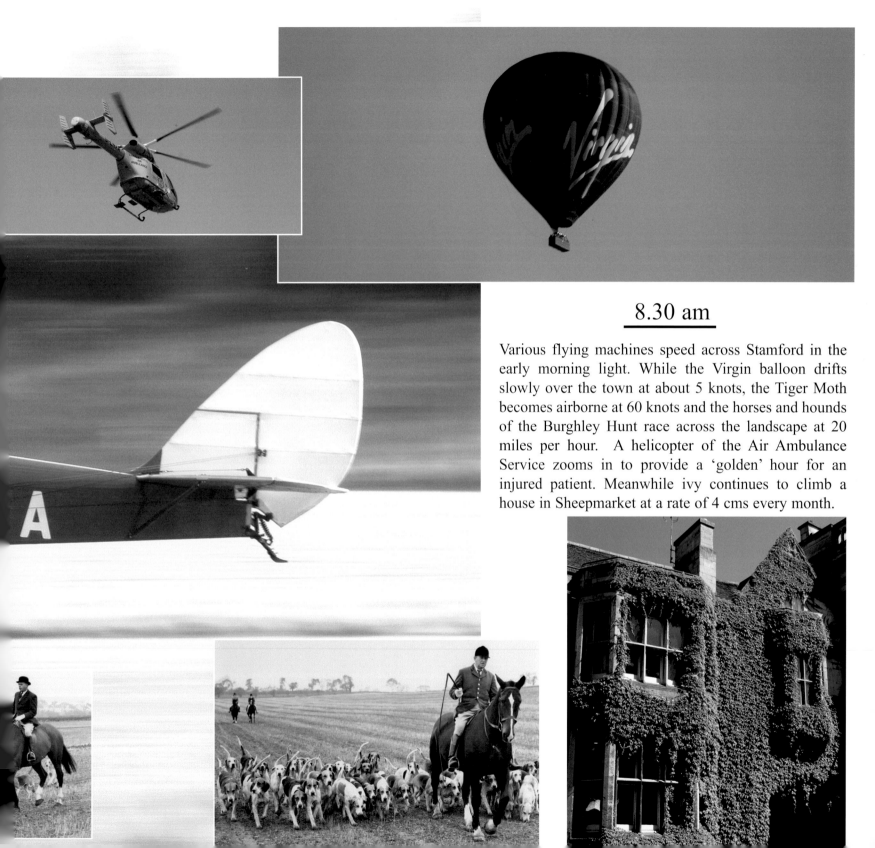

8.30 am

Various flying machines speed across Stamford in the early morning light. While the Virgin balloon drifts slowly over the town at about 5 knots, the Tiger Moth becomes airborne at 60 knots and the horses and hounds of the Burghley Hunt race across the landscape at 20 miles per hour. A helicopter of the Air Ambulance Service zooms in to provide a 'golden' hour for an injured patient. Meanwhile ivy continues to climb a house in Sheepmarket at a rate of 4 cms every month.

8.45 am

The broad view in the old monochrome print, from the top of the tower of St Martin's Church, looks over the beam of the George Hotel, across the River Welland and Town Bridge up the hill to St Mary's Church with St George's Church to the right. To the left, the towers of St John's Church and All Saints' Church are visible.

Chapter 2

Morning

9 am

This aerial view looks down on to Town Bridge and a scene that has hardly changed for hundreds of years. In 1822, Thomas Rowaldson painted the same scene showing a wagon and horses crossing the bridge. A few years earlier, in June 1809, Daniel Lambert, one of the heaviest men in England, died during a visit to Stamford for the horse races being held on Wittering Heath. A wall of his ground floor room at the Waggon & Horses Inn had to be demolished before his body could be removed. The heaviest known man in England was Peter Yarnall of London who weighed in at 58 stone (368 kg). Daniel Lambert weighed 53 stone when he died. He is buried in St Martin's churchyard and it is said that it took 20 men to lower his coffin into the grave.

DANIEL LAMBERT LIES BURIED IN THIS OLD CHURCHYARD OF ST. MARTINS

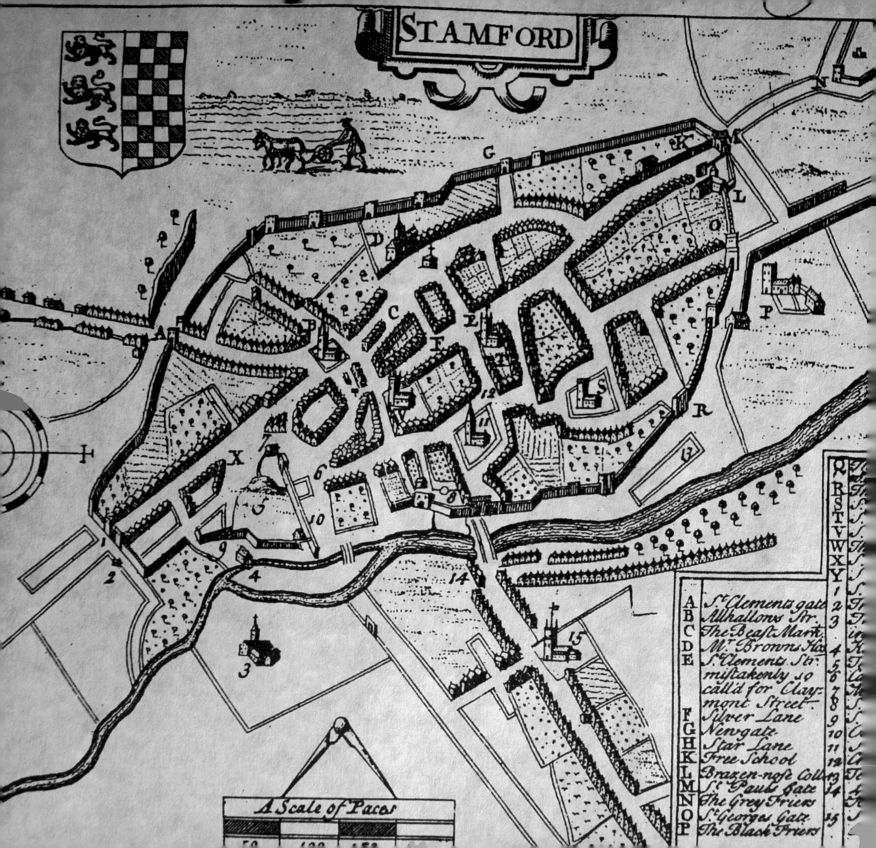

STAMFORD

A Scale of Paces

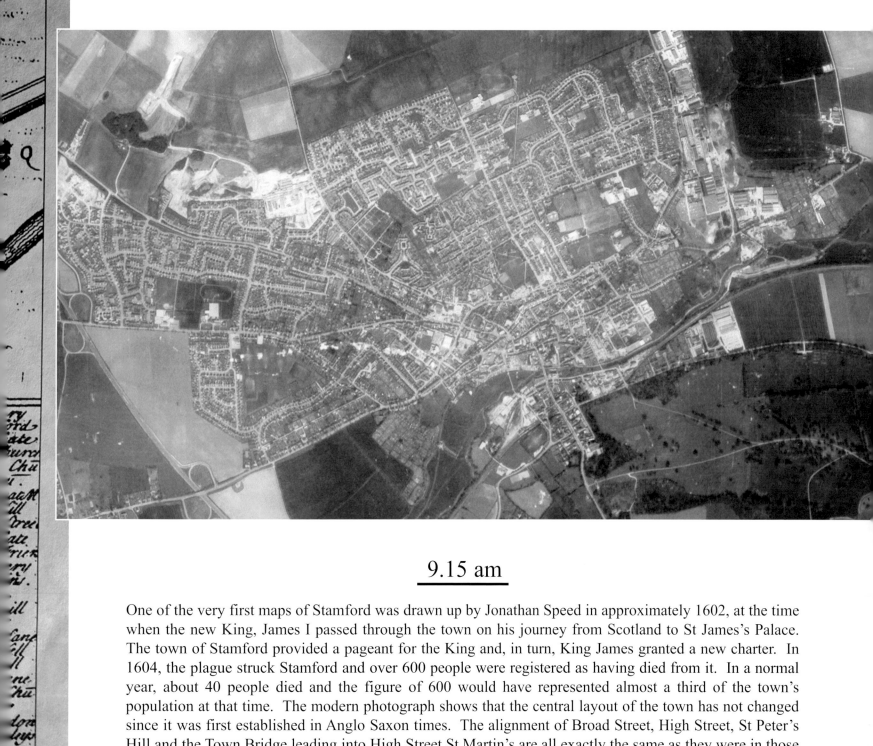

9.15 am

One of the very first maps of Stamford was drawn up by Jonathan Speed in approximately 1602, at the time when the new King, James I passed through the town on his journey from Scotland to St James's Palace. The town of Stamford provided a pageant for the King and, in turn, King James granted a new charter. In 1604, the plague struck Stamford and over 600 people were registered as having died from it. In a normal year, about 40 people died and the figure of 600 would have represented almost a third of the town's population at that time. The modern photograph shows that the central layout of the town has not changed since it was first established in Anglo Saxon times. The alignment of Broad Street, High Street, St Peter's Hill and the Town Bridge leading into High Street St Martin's are all exactly the same as they were in those early days.

9.30 am

The expansive Pavilions sports ground provides green space amongst the housing developments off Empingham Road. Only 4 miles to the north, the Battle of Empingham took place in 1470 when King Edward IV, shown inset, defeated rebel forces lead by Lord Welles. During World War II, long before the new houses were built, the site where the Viking Invader public house now stands was occupied by a POW camp for Italian soldiers. During the war, a teenager named Ron Knight of Great Casterton, now renowned for his restored vintage traction engines, was given permission by his headmaster to be absent from school to help gather in the vital harvest. Ron tells how a lorry arrived at the fields with about 30 Italian POWs but only one guard. His father put him in charge of six of the POWs even though Ron could not speak Italian and none of his 'prisoners' could speak English. However, he showed them what was required and they worked together as a team until the harvest was safely in. After the war, many Italians chose to stay in Stamford which may account for the large number of Italian restaurants in the town.

9.45 am

In 1960 the Stamford bypass was opened, the narrow streets of the town no longer had to cope with the heavy flow of traffic that had previously passed through it. Just west of the A1, where the present boundary between Rutland and Lincolnshire now runs, the old county boundary is still clearly defined by a precise zig-zag of hedgerows across the fields. Stamford's imposing Town Hall was built in 1776, more than 200 years before the A1 bypass was built. The monochrome aerial photograph, to the left, shows crop marks displaying the route of the Roman 'Ermine Street'. This area is now completely covered by modern housing developments.

THE ROMAN FORD

ONE OF THE MOST IMPORTANT ROMAN ROADS
TO THE NORTH, FROM LONDON TO LINCOLN AND
YORK, CROSSED HERE.
IN A.D. 61 SURVIVORS OF THE NINTH ROMAN LEGION
FLED THIS WAY, PURSUED BY QUEEN BOADICEA.
AFTER THE COLLAPSE OF THE BRIDGE, THE LOWER
CROSSING WAS PREFERRED AND STAMFORD GREW
AROUND THIS IN SAXON TIMES

10 am

At 10 am, the River Welland is calm and tranquil. It was at this point that the Roman road, 'Ermine Street', forded the river. This was one of the most important Roman roads connecting London (Londinium), Lincoln (Lindum) and York (Eberacum). In AD 60, the combined tribes of the Iceni, the Catuvellauni and the Coritani joined forces in an attempt to expel the Romans. In AD 61, survivors of the Roman IXth Legion were pursued across this ford, at present day Stamford by the Celtic Queen Boudicca, known by the Romans as Queen Boadicea.

10.15 am

The 'South Prospect of Stamford' clearly shows the various buildings and churches in the town of Stamford. Many kings and queens visited the town; King Henry VIII in 1528, 1532 & 1539; Queen Elizabeth I dined at Whitefriars in 1566, King James I on his way from Scotland in 1602 and Charles I in 1633 & 1634. During her reign, Queen Elizabeth II has visited the town on both formal and informal occasions, especially to see the Burghley Horse Trials.

10.30 am

Neatly laid out caravans, gathered for their annual rally, show measured precision across the green lawns of Burghley Park. A body of redcoats march out of St George's Square while overhead, the Red Arrows perform a fly past en route to an airshow.

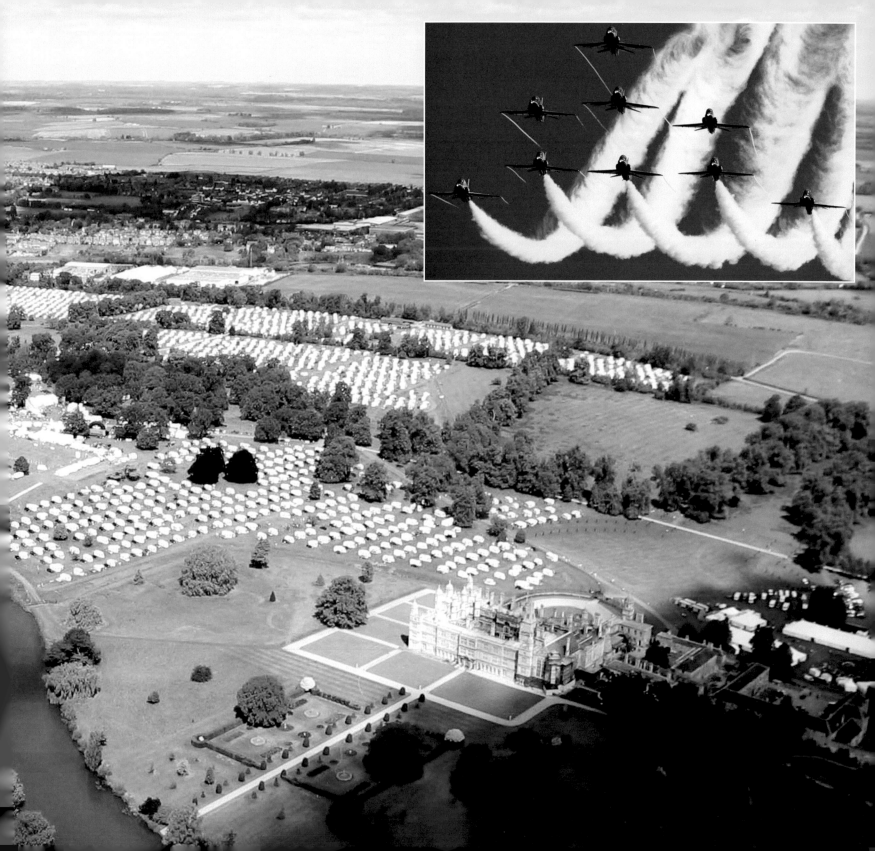

10.45 am

By 10.45 am, Stamford's town centre is already busy. The church, in the centre of the aerial photo, is St Marys Church situated at the top of the hill above the Town Hall and the Town Bridge. The Town Crier, in his bright red uniform, stands outside the window of the Mayor's Parlour. On the Meadows, two Hussars take part in a period re-enactment. At top right is an undated monochrome photograph taken from the roof of the Town Hall showing the flooded Meadows beyond the roof tops.

11 am

In the late morning, both cygnets and skateboarders enjoy freedom of movement - one down the hill and one up the river. The 'Stamford Spitfire' enjoyed the freedom of the skies above Lincolnshire during World War II. Like many towns and cities, the people of Stamford collected £5,000 pounds and paid for a Spitfire. The Mk IIB Spitfire, registration number P8505 shown inset at left complete with coat of arms, was one of a thousand Spitfires built at Castle Bromwich. It entered service on 3rd June 1941 with Number 222 (Natal) Squadron based at Matlask in Norfolk. On 4th September, the 'Stamford' Spitfire was transferred to Number 266 (Rhodesia) Squadron based at Kings Cliffe and then joined Number 65 (East India) Squadron based at Kirton Lindsey in its own county, Lincolnshire. The 'Stamford' Spitfire was lost in a mid-air collision on 12th June 1943 when the pilot, Flying Officer O'Reilly of the Royal Australian Air Force, was killed. The aircraft made a vital contribution to the war effort during its operational life before it was superseded by the more advanced versions of the Spitfire as shown above.

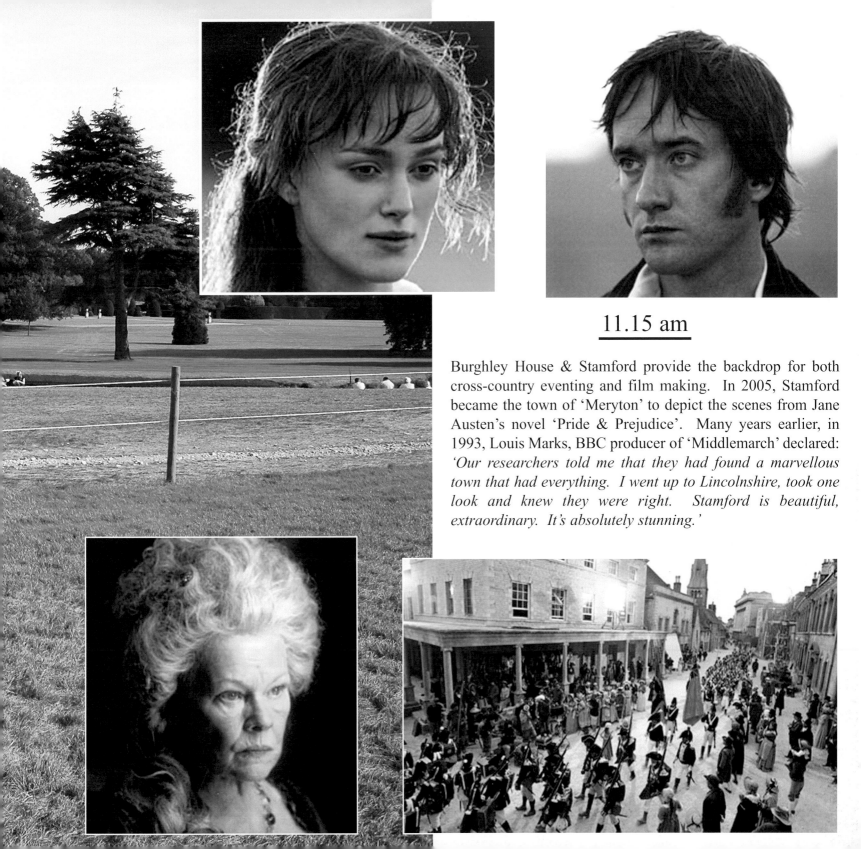

11.15 am

Burghley House & Stamford provide the backdrop for both cross-country eventing and film making. In 2005, Stamford became the town of 'Meryton' to depict the scenes from Jane Austen's novel 'Pride & Prejudice'. Many years earlier, in 1993, Louis Marks, BBC producer of 'Middlemarch' declared: *'Our researchers told me that they had found a marvellous town that had everything. I went up to Lincolnshire, took one look and knew they were right. Stamford is beautiful, extraordinary. It's absolutely stunning.'*

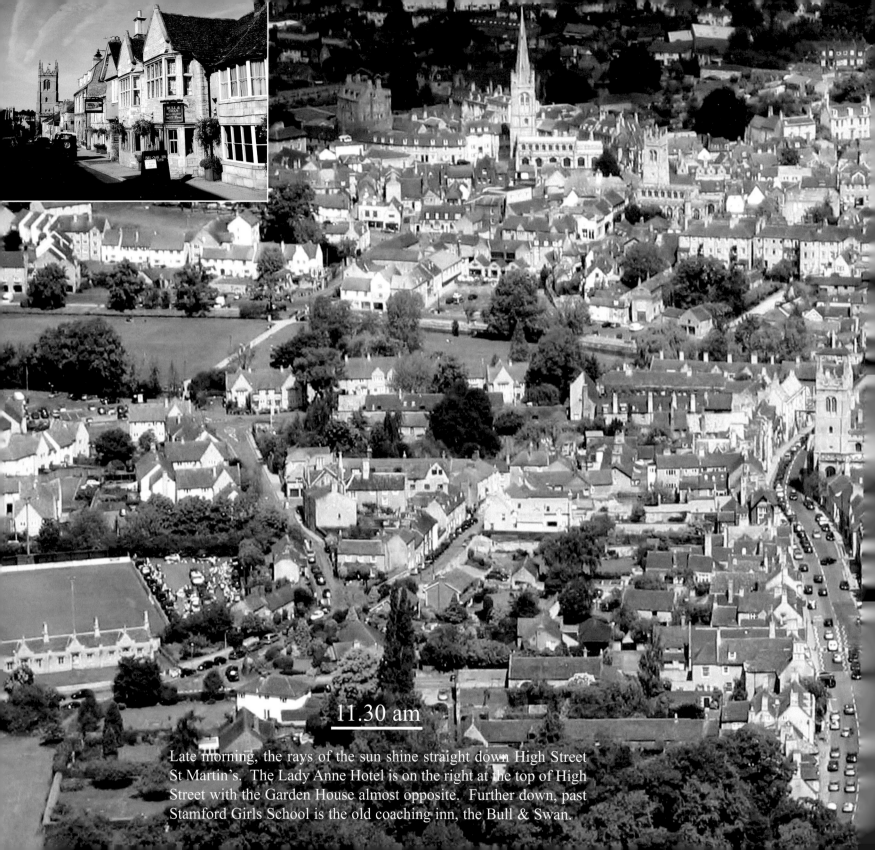

11.30 am

Late morning, the rays of the sun shine straight down High Street St Martin's. The Lady Anne Hotel is on the right at the top of High Street with the Garden House almost opposite. Further down, past Stamford Girls School is the old coaching inn, the Bull & Swan.

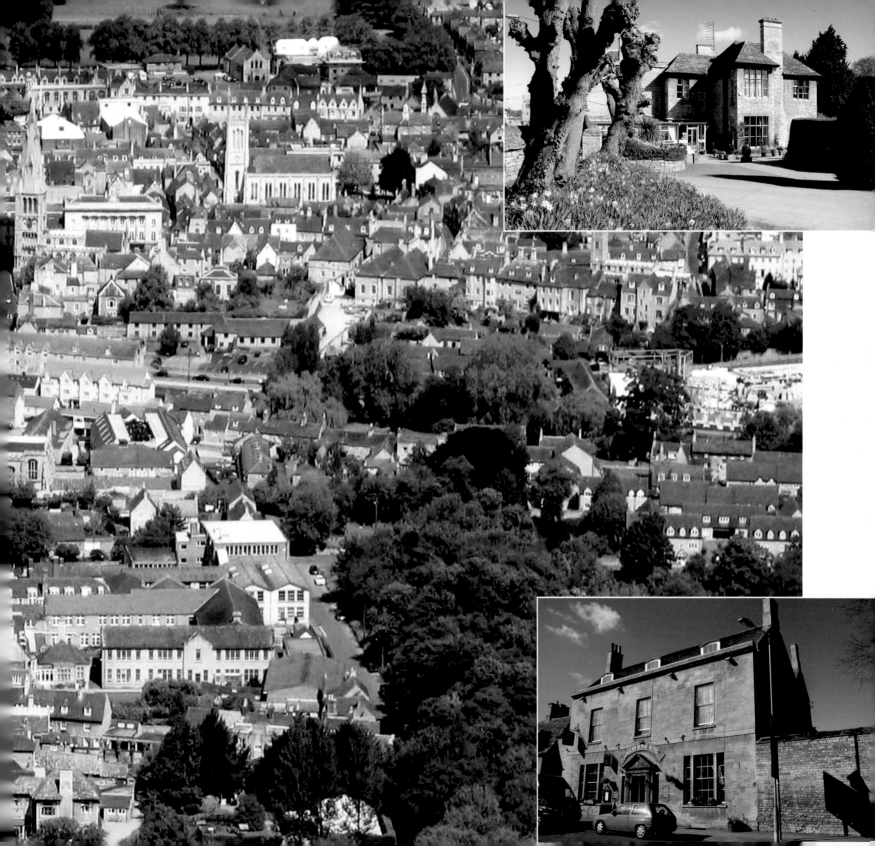

11.45 am

Burghley House was built and mostly designed by William Cecil, Lord High Treasurer to Queen Elizabeth I, between 1555 and 1587. Queen Elizabeth I did visit Stamford and although a bedroom was prepared for her, she did not stay at Burghley due to a smallpox outbreak there. In 1962, Queen Elizabeth II visited Stamford and was escorted during her visit by Lord Burghley. He had won a gold medal over the hurdles at the Amsterdam Olympics in 1928.

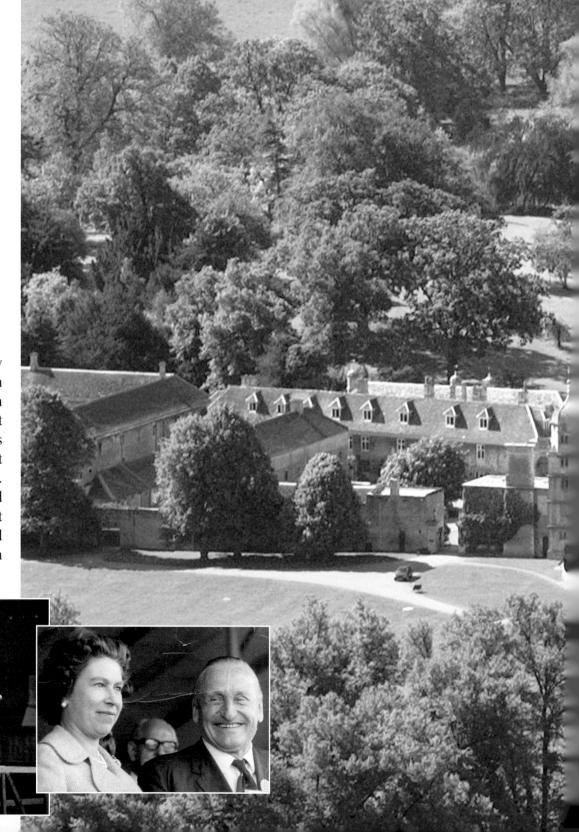

Chapter 3

Midday

<u>12 noon</u>

At midday the sun is almost directly overhead and floods over the centre of Stamford where a market has been held since medieval times. The twelve o'clock train stands ready to depart from Stamford station on its way to Oakham, Leicester and Birmingham whilst the Tiger Moth waits for a refuel at Sibson airfield. The inset picture shows that the corner of All Saints Street has changed little over the years.

12.15 pm

The restored houses at the old Sheepmarket stand pristine in the clear midday light. In the garden of the Northfields public house, Mayor John Judge takes a passive but active part in fund raising for the Mayor's charity.

12.30 pm

From above details are revealed that are not visible to the observer on the ground. The crowded area where the Stamford Mercury, the oldest newspaper in England, has its modern offices, is surrounded by quaint narrow lanes that house all manner of small businesses. Behind the newspaper's offices lies the River Welland and the Freemen's Meadow.

12.45 pm

The Castle Cement plant stands behind the combined villages of Ketton, Geeston and Aldgate, where the key ingredient, limestone, is readily available. The Castle Cement company is planting thousands of new trees around their quarries to conserve and protect the environment. In the foreground of the main picture is Ketton Hall surrounded by trees, and to the right, the towering spire of the 13th century church. Roger de Ketton, who was born here in 1143 AD, went on the crusades and later translated the Arabic theories of algebra and alchemy into English.

1 pm

Two hundred years ago, the markets in Stamford would close by 1 pm and the farmers would return to their farms. Blackfriars Priory, where the present Stamford & Rutland Hospital is situated marked the edge of the town. At that time there were no houses in the area called 'Northfields'. On their way home farmers would gather for a final glass of beer at the last cottage in town - a place that became known as the 'Parting Pot Cottage'. Modern houses and schools, including Stamford College, were built across the 'Northfields' in the 1960s.

1.15 pm

Redcoats gather for an ale outside the half timbered inn called 'St Marys Vaults'. Below, on the Meadows, a mounted soldier of the Napoleonic era takes part in a ceremonial display. Above, in Broad Street, the outside of the buildings have changed little since that time.

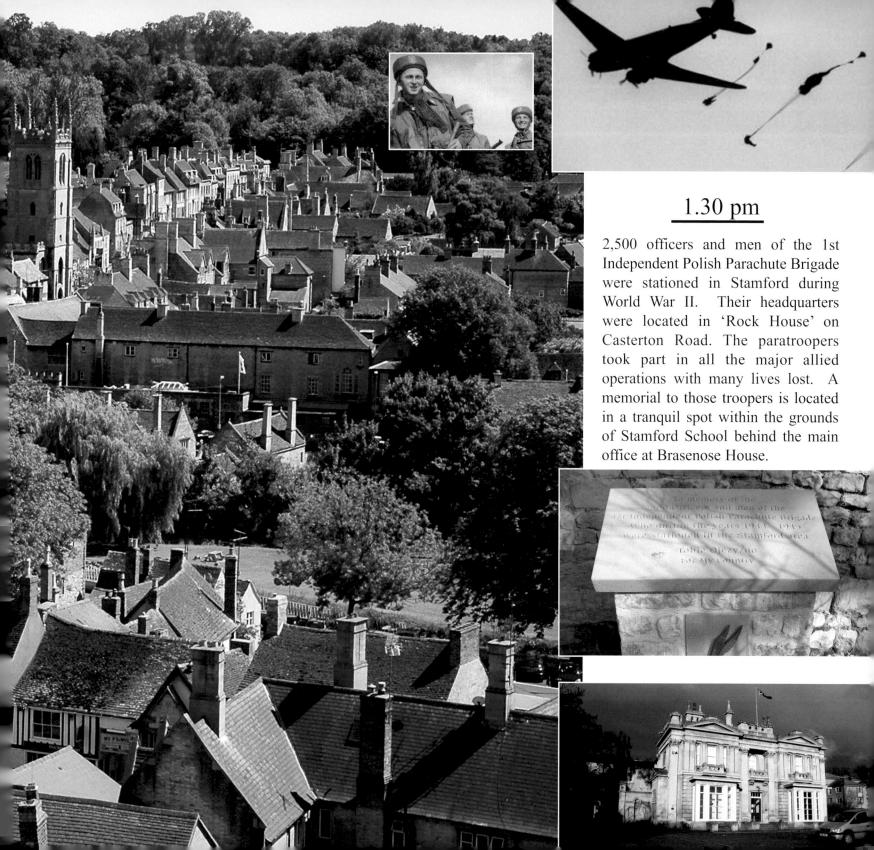

1.30 pm

2,500 officers and men of the 1st Independent Polish Parachute Brigade were stationed in Stamford during World War II. Their headquarters were located in 'Rock House' on Casterton Road. The paratroopers took part in all the major allied operations with many lives lost. A memorial to those troopers is located in a tranquil spot within the grounds of Stamford School behind the main office at Brasenose House.

1.45 pm

In the early afternoon, a musical & whimsical re-enactment of the slaying of the dragon by St George takes place in front of the Tuscan portico of Stamford Library. The troupe of Morris dancers are based in Bourne but are a familiar sight in Stamford. St George is the patron saint of England and St George's Day is celebrated throughout England on 23rd April, two days after the birthdate of Queen Elizabeth II who was born on 21st April 1926.

HERE STOOD ST. PETER'S GATE
DISMANTLED IN 1770.
ON THE SOUTH WAS BUILT AND
ENDOWED THE SAME YEAR
HOPKIN'S HOSPITAL BY
JOHN HOPKINS THE THEN MAYOR.
THE TOWER OR BASTION SOME
THIRTY YARDS TO THE NORTH
IN WEST STREET IS THE ONLY
ONE NOW STANDING.

2 pm

The early afternoon light falls on St Peter's Gate and Rutland Terrace where the last bastion of the walls of Stamford still stands. St Peter's Gate was dismantled in 1770 and Hopkin's Hospital, to the south of the gate, was built the following year by John Hopkins, Mayor of Stamford at that time.

2.15 pm

The hand-tinted photograph of the busy Broad Street market was taken in 1953 at the time of Queen Elizabeth II's coronation. The photographer was positioned at the highest point of Browne's Hospital. Equally busy today, is the road which passes the George Hotel, crosses the Town Bridge and up to St Marys Church

2.30 pm

Before the bypass was completed, the main A1 known as the Great North Road, ran straight through Stamford. Detective Sergeant Charles Watkinson was stationed here and described the traffic situation: "The traffic was tightly packed and I have ascribed this to the entry and exit of Red Lion Square in the town centre. Southbound traffic arriving here was faced with the need to get into and down St John's Street, a narrow street that would not easily allow two heavy vehicles to pass. Usually, there was a uniformed officer in Red Lion Square and his signals, sometimes unconventional and not in any Police manuals, were obeyed by the drivers. On Xmas Eve, Constable Pike was given a cigar by a passing heavy goods driver for all his help through the year."

2.45 pm

Only Freemen could trade in Stamford in the 18th & 19th centuries. In the 1871 Enclosure Act, the Freemen of Stamford were given the Meadows as grazing land for their cattle. One was either born the son of a Freeman or like Sir Malcolm Sargent, made an honourary Freeman. With only six Freemen remaining in Stamford, cattle are no longer grazed on the Meadows. Today the Meadows are open to all, including players in a vintage cricket match.

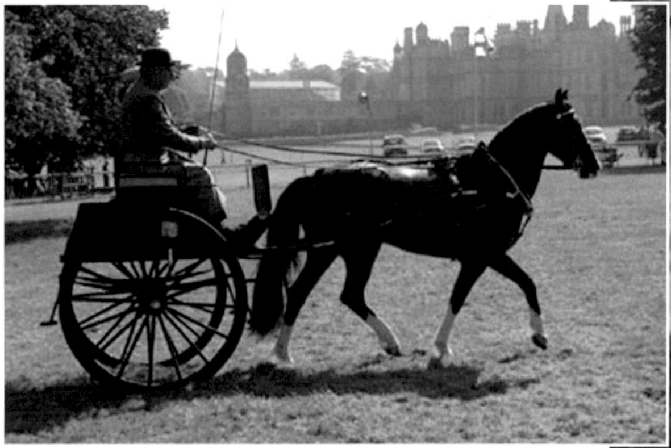

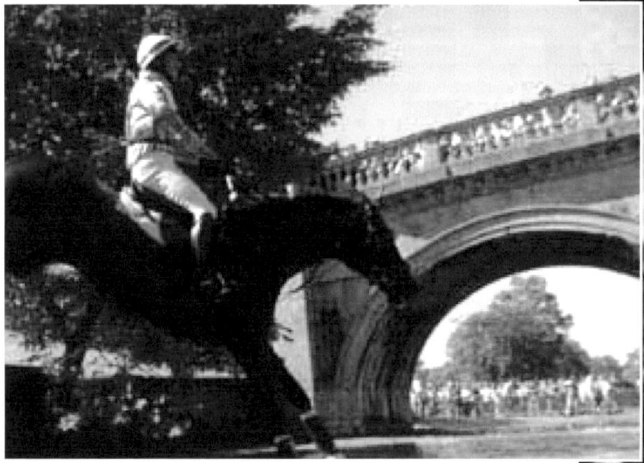

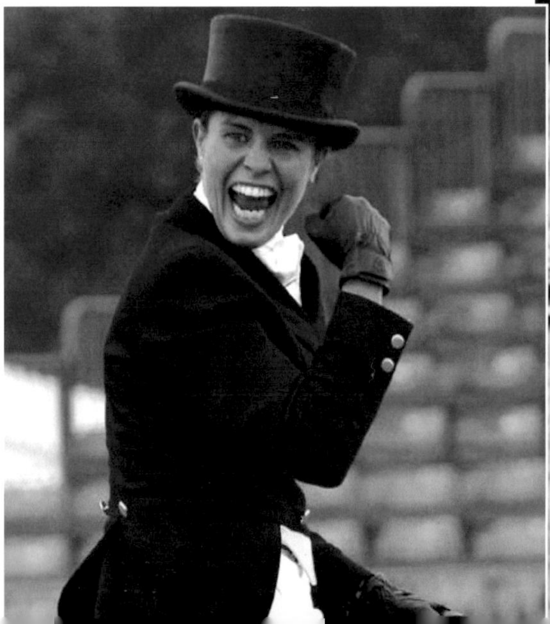

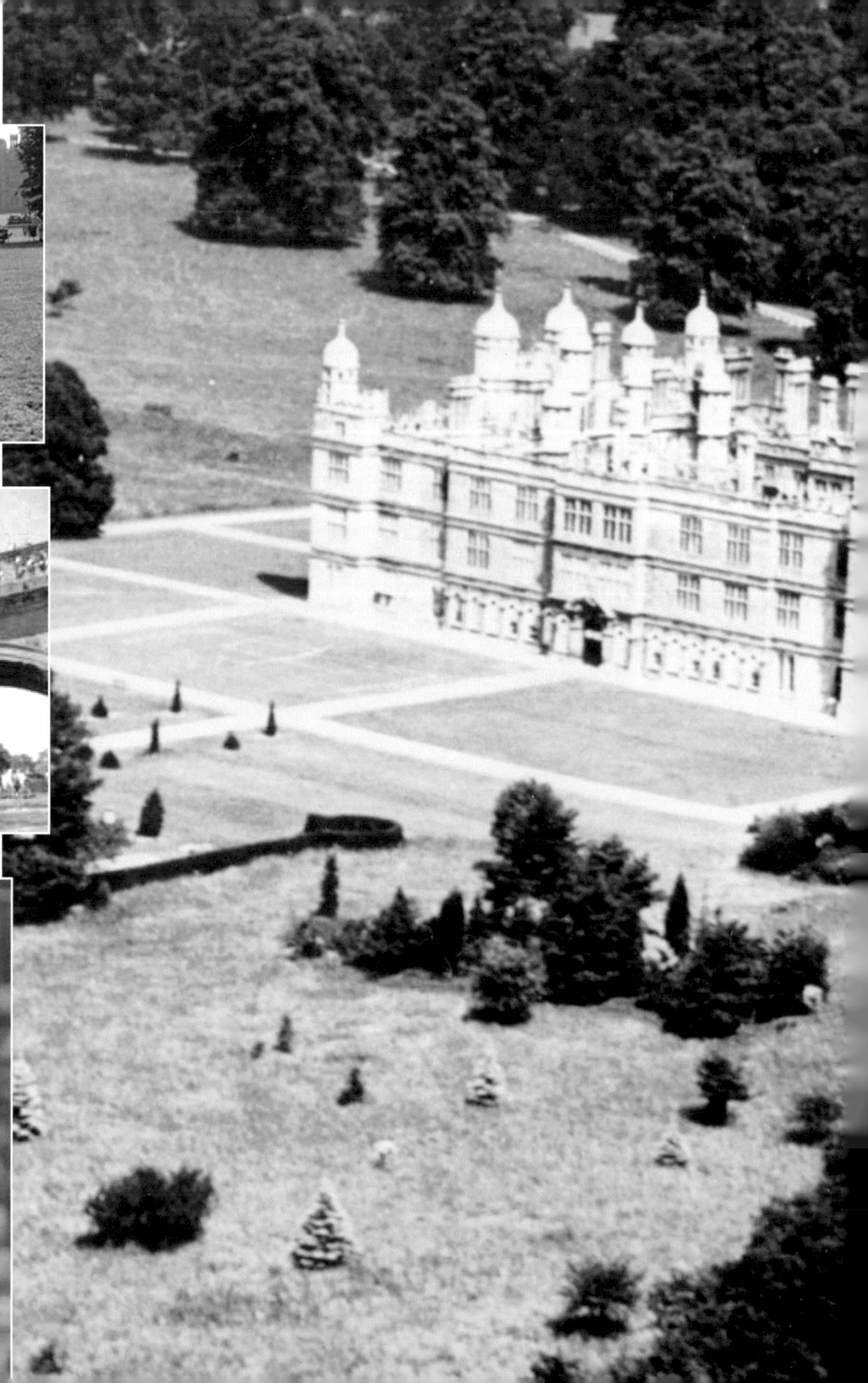

3 pm

By mid-afternoon, one of the premier English horse trials (the other is Badmington) is in full swing. The trials originally marked the start of the hunting season. A formation of RAF Harrier jets from nearby Wittering, fly past to mark the opening of the three day event. This culminates in the arduous cross country trial and the awarding of prizes to proud and often exhilarated winners. The original monochrome aerial photograph of Burghley House was taken on 7th July 1918 when an American jazz band played in the grounds.

3.15 pm

Normally, in the mid afternoon, a football match would be in full swing on the Daniels ground beyond the Meadows and the railway station. When this photograph was taken, it was late summer and the only occupant is the groundsman cutting the grass of the football pitch. To the right of the main picture, cricket is being played on the Stamford Endowed Schools pitch while a well drilled band marches through Red Lion Square.

3.30 pm

Shadows begin to creep across the grass towards the imposing entrance Burghley Park on the old Great North Road. This entrance, known as t 'Bottle Lodges', was built by William Legg in 1801 and is just before top of High Street St Martin's, with its view of Stamford that was captur by the artists Turner and Walter Scott. In both paintings, the buildings Stamford High School are visible. Visitors have always been impress with the view of the town from this vantage point. On the other side town, the school clock strikes 3.30 pm. What once was St Paul's Churc now used as the chapel for The Stamford Endowed Schools.

3.45 pm

The mid afternoon light falls on the village of Ryhall where a modern fish farm is prominent at the bottom of the photograph. Saint Tibba and Saint Ebba lived in Ryhall 700 years ago. A well, named after St Ebba, existed on the side of the hill above the ford. Hence 'St Ebba's well ford' became 'Stablesford'. In the years before the bridge was built this ford was the safest way to cross the river. Against a backdrop of tall mature trees, a rider clears the 'Mushroom' fence en route to the Land Rover water splash.

Chapter 4

Afternoon

4 pm

In the quiet of the late afternoon, different house styles contrast along St Peter's Street and Barn Hill where King Charles I spent his last night as a free man.

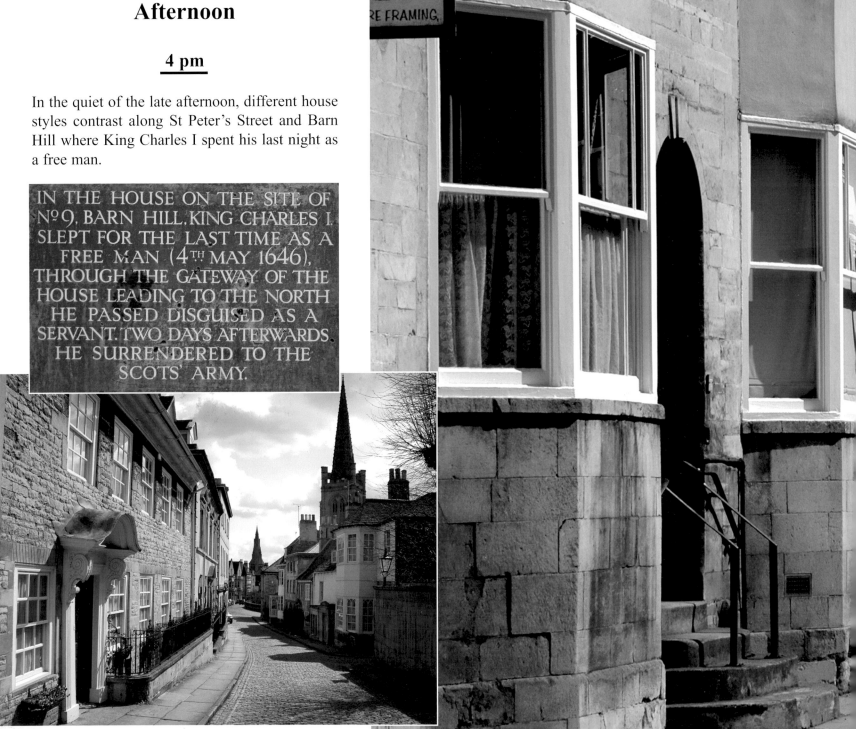

IN THE HOUSE ON THE SITE OF Nº 9, BARN HILL, KING CHARLES I. SLEPT FOR THE LAST TIME AS A FREE MAN (4ᵀᴴ MAY 1646), THROUGH THE GATEWAY OF THE HOUSE LEADING TO THE NORTH HE PASSED DISGUISED AS A SERVANT. TWO DAYS AFTERWARDS HE SURRENDERED TO THE SCOTS' ARMY.

4.15 pm

After the invasion in 1066, King William ordered a listing of all his new possessions in a document that became known as 'The Domesday Book'. In 1086, there were only two towns of note in Lincolnshire, Lincoln itself and Stamford. This period marked the beginning of a glorious era for Stamford; in trading, in manufacturing and, dramatically, in ecclesiastical and educational terms. Today, opposite the Town Hall, this Norman arch still stands at the entrance to one of the cobbled passageways leading down to the river.

4.30 pm

Punting during the late afternoon on the River Welland adjacent to the location where small trading fen barges used to dock at the Stamford quays. The excellent lines of communications along the Great North Road and along the navigable River Welland to the Wash and the North Sea ensured that the wool trade from Stamford was a success. However, the river silted up and although it was dredged, it eventually silted up completely and the trade ceased.

4.45 pm

The late afternoon light falls on the changing face of Stamford. St Leonards Priory is hidden by mature trees only a few steps away from the modern roundabout that leads to Morrisons supermarket where the lure of readily available, free parking has drawn shoppers away from the quaint passages off Red Lion Square.

5 pm

Young ladies dance around the maypole between the showers whilst the strong, late afternoon sunlight floods across Wittering and Stamford. An RAF Harrier thunders down the wet runway while lightning strikes the upper stories of Burghley House. The house was built on rock and when the lightning conductors were installed, the builders had problems finding a 12 foot depth of soil required to discharge any strikes - not even 3 feet of soil was available. The problem was solved by using six horizontal copper sheets buried beneath the shallow soil. To the north of Stamford, a rainbow arcs over houses on Ryhall Road while down by the River Welland, ducks shelter beneath the footbridge.

5.15 pm

By late afternoon, the sun is sparkling from the west front of Burghley House, which was added in 1577. The shadows deepen in the lee of the George Hotel, famous as a coaching inn for hundreds of years. Before the railways were built, sixty coaches passed through Stamford every day. Inset is a drawing of the Regent Coach which departed from London at six o'clock in the morning and reached Stamford less than 12 hours later at a quarter to six in the evening - a remarkable journey over poor roads. The JCB contender was tested at RAF Wittering before gaining the world land speed record for diesel-powered vehicles in Utah, with an average speed of 328.767 mph (529 kph). If it was possible for this car to travel on the original coach route from London to the George today, it would complete the journey in just 19 minutes.

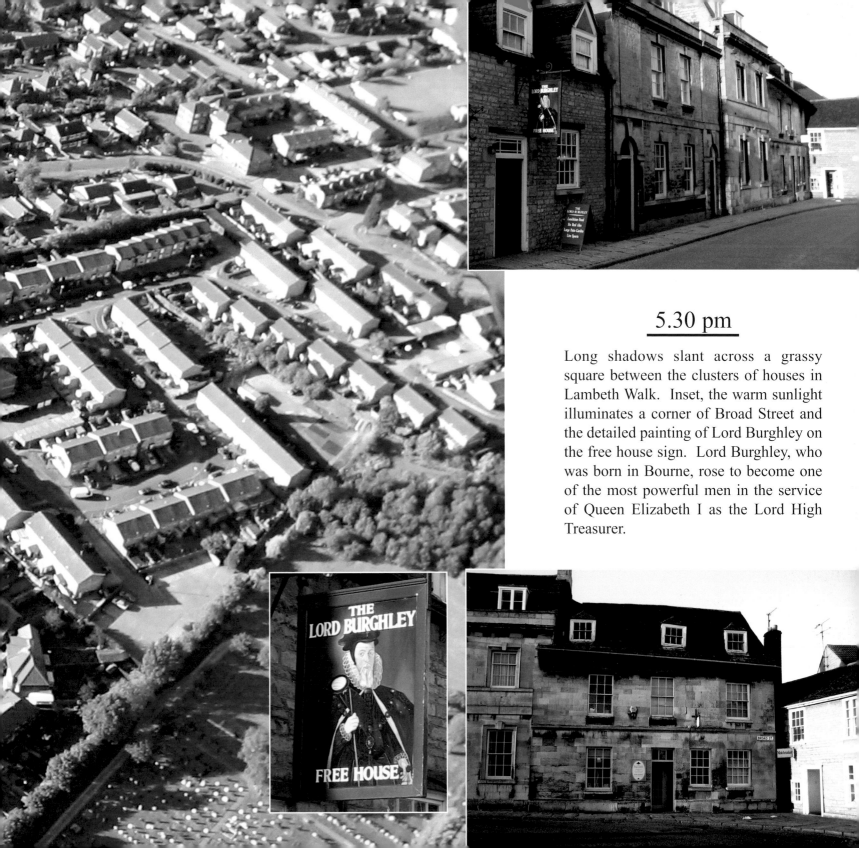

5.30 pm

Long shadows slant across a grassy square between the clusters of houses in Lambeth Walk. Inset, the warm sunlight illuminates a corner of Broad Street and the detailed painting of Lord Burghley on the free house sign. Lord Burghley, who was born in Bourne, rose to become one of the most powerful men in the service of Queen Elizabeth I as the Lord High Treasurer.

5.45 pm

The late afternoon sun floods over the converted Newstead and Hudds Mill which contrast with the colourful modern houses of Rutland Heights, so-called since part of this estate is within the county boundary of Rutland. Across the A1 is a strangely shaped hedgerow, shown on page 46, dividing two fields that once marked the old boundary between Lincolnshire and Rutland.

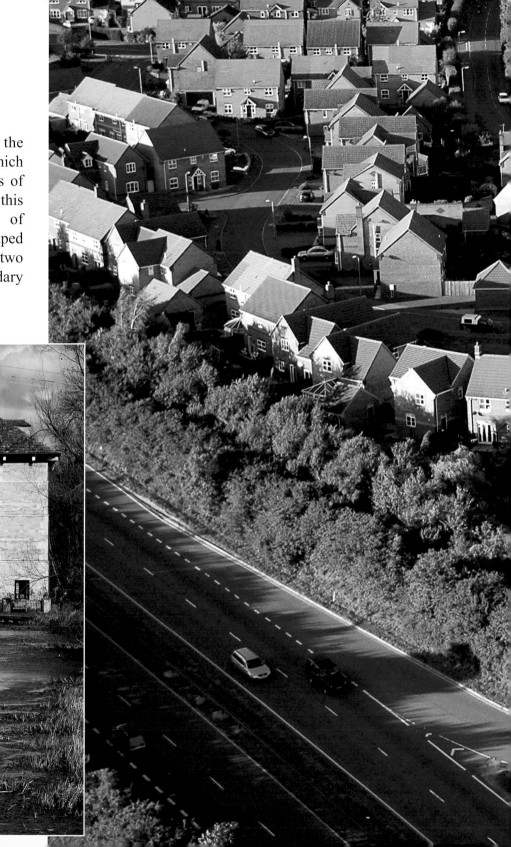

6 pm

The sunburst centrepiece is the focal point of a memorial wood and garden which was established by the people of Stamford in memory of the life and work of Diana, Princess of Wales. She was born on the Sandringham Estate on 1st July 1961 and died in a car crash on 31st August 1997. The garden is of a cruciform shape and incorporates indigenous trees and shrubs. The sunburst sculpture was commissioned from Antony Poels. He incorporated original artwork by pupils from Stamford Primary School into his finished design, which is positioned to catch the last rays of the setting sun in an area of quiet reflection. Some of the oak trees in the park, where the deer graze unperturbed by visitors, have been standing

6.15 pm

In 1756, the 9th Earl commissioned 'Capability' Brown to lay out the park that surrounds Burghley House which is now home to a magnificent herd of fallow deer. To the north, on the other side of Stamford is Tolthorpe Hall, shown inset, widely regarded as Europe's finest open air theatre, set in the grounds of an historic country house. More than 30,000 theatre lovers visit each season to enjoy a picnic and a play. The Stamford Shakespeare Company used to hold its open air performances in the Monastery Garden at the George Hotel before moving to Tolthorpe in 1976. During the production of 'A Midsummer Night's Dream', a specially constructed stage set allows the king and queen of the fairies, Oberon and Titania, to fly down unexpectedly from the tree tops over the open air stage and into the dream sequence of the play.

6.30 pm

During the past five hundred years, there were many windmills and watermills in and around Stamford. Today this abandoned windmill on the hill above Ketton is one of the few remaining in the area. One of the balloons drifts by in the distance as the last rays of the sun shine on the ruined windmill. The Stamford coat of arms, carved high on the side of the Town Hall, and the deer herd at Burghley are both caught in the last light of day. In Burghley Park, the winner of the cross country event is interviewed in the shadow of the trees.

6.45 pm

The strong, lowering sun sends a long sunpath down the river, silhouetting a canoeist at the end of his journey. Many years ago, the River Welland was navigable all the way from the Wash to this point. Inset, two canoeists paddle close to where the fen barges once docked. This spot is now where the public house, 'Quayhole Kates' is situated.

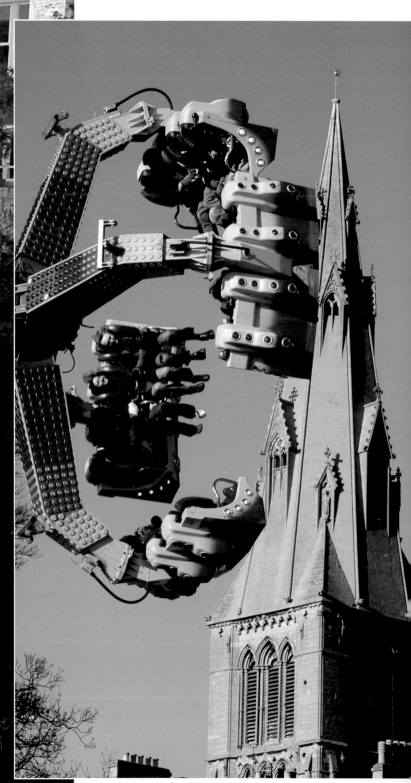

7 pm

The last rays of the sun illuminate the rustic red foliage alongside the River Welland. Two swans, the male known as a 'cob' and the female known as a 'pen', cruise slowly downriver to their nesting place. The majestic swan is the largest and most beautiful of the waterfowl family. Both Ancient Britons and the Anglo-Saxons believed that a swan's wings sang with a human voice whilst in flight. Also flying and screaming with delight, during the Mid Lent Fair, are riders in a whirling experience called 'The Grab'.

The balloons start their final descent as the sun touches the horizon and disappears from view. In the fading light, the herds of deer wander peacefully across the park as the formation of foot soldiers dismiss and lovers kiss.

7.30 pm

A farmer continues to work into the fading light while, only a few miles to the south, the lights of Stamford Fair whirl the night away. The birds eye view at right shows the filming of 'Middlemarch' in the trasformed St Georges Square in the Stamford location which Louis Marks described as 'absolutley stunning'. The farmer will work on into the night, harvesting in the moonlight, while the revellers party into the dawn and the start of another 'Day Above Stamford'.

Many, many people were involved in making a success of this project and we would like to thank the following; first, our thanks to Lady Victoria Leatham of Burghley House who kindly wrote the foreword; former Mayor John Judge, who wrote the introduction, and archivist Bob Williams, for their invaluable help including access to the archives, use of the paintings in the Town Hall and permission to use the Coat of Arms of Stamford on the title page. Our thanks to Jon Culverhouse, Curator of the Burghley House Collection (pages 62 insets, 88, 107 inset), the late James Meads (pages 36 & 37 insets) and Janet Wright. Special thanks to Sgt James Stewart, formerly of RAF Wittering for detailed research and photograph (Page 56 inset) of the 'Stamford Spitfire'; Geoff O'Connor and Peter Kemp of the Imperial War Museum (pages 56, 76 & 88 insets). The photographs of the Royal Air Force are British Crown copyright reproduced with the permission of the Controller of Her Britannic Majesty's Stationary Office; thanks

also to Gordon Bartley, British Aerospace for the Harrier & Hawk pictures (page 89 inset). Special thanks to Canon Neil Russell of All Saints Church who kindly assisted my son William and me to make the quite difficult ascent of the spire that led to the front cover. It was a pleasure to fly with the following aviators Philip and Susan Shotbolt in the WWII vintage Auster; the balloonists - Alan Lusty, Miles and Helen of Aerographics; Ian and Denise Warrington and Peter Foot; Lucy Kimbell & Frank McClurg of the Northamptonshire School of Flying, Sibson Aerodrome. Introductory trial lessons, on a flight over Stamford are available in the vintage Tiger Moth. The telephone number of the club i 01832 280289, www.nsof.co.uk Special thanks to the lovely people who loaned the punt to we complete strangers (see page 100). We enjoyed the company of fellow photographers and artists; Joe Wright & Alex Bailey, Universal Picture

Published with the support and encouragement of;

HEIDELBERGCEMENT Group

KELHAMS

SOLICITORS and NOTARIES

insets page 59); Ben Howe; Rex Needle from Bourne - see his fascinating web page www.bourne-lincs.org.uk (inset page 19); John Smith (page 126); Bruce Barnett and JCB PR; Derek at Air team - see their excellent web site www.airteamimages.com; E.J. Van Koningsveld (Page 53 insets); Graham Cooke MBE GAvA, co-founder of the Guild of Fine Artists for his painting of the Virgin balloon lifting off from the Meadows (page 24/25); Amanda Lewis; Kit Houghton (pages 88/89 insets); Rikki of Northfields (page 84); Chris & Sarah Hollobon; Richard Insall (inset page 124) and Derek Harrison at the Stamford Shakespeare Company. Thanks to the family support of Marc & Patrick in London; Robert, Kerri, William and Max in Houston plus Nicholas in Washington; Robert Nowell's photographs (page 15, 23); thanks to Simone (for editing the book), Cyrus, Isa & newly arrived Layla; William Nowell (who also poled the punt and designed the book). Finally, this book could not have been published without the help and encouragement of Andy Stretton of Stamford Photo Express (Page 8/9 by the late Richard Lakey); Peter Weller, David Bagshaw and Danny Daniels of Castle Cement; all at Kelhams solicitors and notaries, with especial thanks to Roger Vipan with his charity driving experiences in his Ferrari; Suzanne Moon of the Rutland & Stamford Mercury for unstinting support (Pages 28, 30, 34, 40, 48). In turn, it is our pleasure to support the Lincolnshire & Nottinghamshire Air Ambulance Service and the efforts of Peter Aldrick, Maggie Woodward and Vivienne Chambers, by contributing £1/- from every book sold. It costs £1,000/- every time the helicopter is called out and the service relies totally on donations from the public.

Our thanks to you all.

John and Christine Nowell,
Stamford, Lincolnshire.

Rutland & Stamford Mercury

Stamford Express Photo

John met Christine at the swimming pool at RAF Changi in Singapore when he joined 205 Squadron and Christine was convalescing after a minor operation. They now have six children and four grandchildren. John completed his first solo in a glider over Lincolnshire at the age of 16 before he joined the Royal Air Force and flew with 206, 205 and 230 Squadrons, some of the old flying boat squadrons. The records of the early exploration flights from England to New Zealand and Cape Town were the basis of his 'Now & Then' series of books. His first book in the 'Day Above' series, 'A Day Above Oman' has been reprinted 14 times. His discovery of 5,000 year-old, perfectly preserved tombs in Oman led to a Fellowship of the Royal Geographic Society. Christine's first book was 'Now & Then - Abu Dhabi'. This book, 'A Day Above Stamford', is John's 15th book. Their next projects are 'A Day Above Malta', 'A Day Above Lincolnshire', "A Day Above The Lake District' and a corporate book, 'A Day Above Ribblesdale'.

Other books in the series or by the authors.

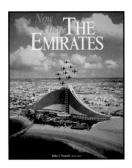
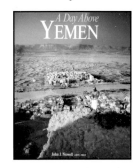
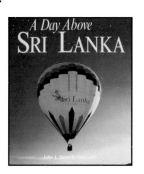

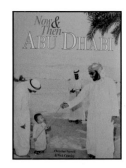

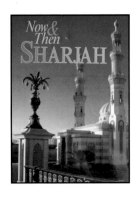

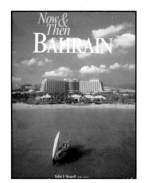
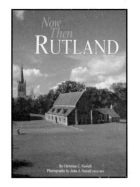